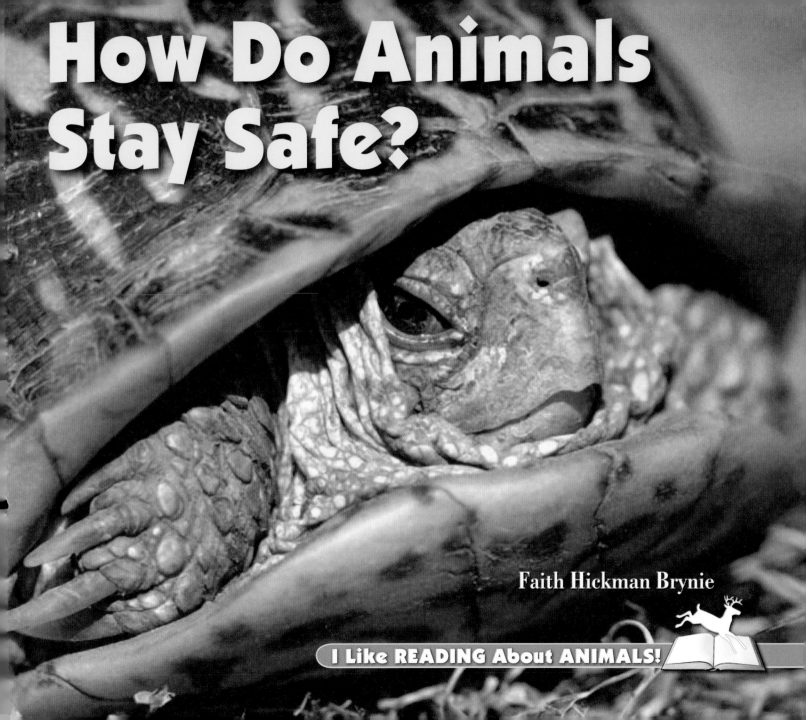

How Do Animals Stay Safe?

Faith Hickman Brynie

I Like READING About ANIMALS!

Contents

Note to Parents and Teachers: The *I Like Reading About Animals!* series supports the National Science Education Standards for K–4 science. The Words to Know section introduces subject-specific vocabulary words for the two different reading levels presented in this book (new reader and fluent reader), including pronunciation and definitions. Early readers may need help with these new words.

Words to Know

New Readers

herd (HURD)—A group of animals that are all the same kind.

poison (POY zuhn)—A chemical that causes harm to living things.

quill (KWIL)—A long, thin, pointy spine on an animal's body.

Fluent Readers

disguise (dihs GUYZ)—To change the way one looks in order to hide.

mouth brooder—A fish that carries its eggs in its mouth until they hatch and the young are ready to live on their own.

predator (PREH duh tur)—An animal that hunts other animals for food.

Staying Safe

◀ This tortoise pulls its body into its shell. The shell keeps it safe. Many other animals do not have shells. They have to hide or find other ways to stay safe.

How do animals protect themselves?

Most animals are not protected by a shell as a tortoise is. Some can hide. Others have ways of fighting back—or, at least, of looking fierce.

You can see an example here. The toad stands tall and puffs up its body. It looks too big and scary for the grass snake to eat!

Let's look at some more animals and how they stay safe.

How do sloths stay safe?

This baby tree sloth holds onto its mother. Tree sloths move slowly. Their fur looks like tree bark. This helps them hide in trees.

▶

How do tree sloths hide or fight?

When a sloth curls up in a ball, it looks like a termite nest or a knot in the wood of a tree. When it hides in a tree, its body is the same colors as the branches. Predators, such as the jaguar and the harpy eagle, cannot see a sloth hiding in the crook of a tree.

When tree sloths cannot hide, they fight. They have sharp claws. They can bite. They also have a good sense of smell. They know when an enemy is coming before it gets too close.

What is in this fish's mouth?

This jawfish has eggs in his mouth. He keeps them safe there. Soon the eggs will hatch in his mouth. They will become tiny jawfish.

What is a mouth brooder?

Fish that keep their eggs in their mouths are called **mouth brooders**. When jawfish mate, the female lays the eggs in burrows in the sand or in spaces between the rocks. The male takes the eggs in his mouth. He keeps them there except when he eats. Then he hides them in the burrow or in the rocks.

After his meal, he goes back to get the eggs. He continues mouth brooding. When the eggs hatch, he lets the young fish swim away.

Why do skunks raise their tails?

Danger! A bobcat is near. It wants to eat the skunk. ▷
The skunk raises its tail. It sprays a bad smell.
The bobcat runs away. The skunk is safe.

Why do predators run away from skunks?

A skunk's spray makes most animals sick to their stomach. It also burns their eyes. Skunks can spray as far as 6 to 9 feet (2 or 3 meters). Predators learn to keep their distance.

The skunk's smell does not bother some animals. Some large birds hunt and kill skunks for food. Great horned owls and red-tailed hawks eat skunks.

What are these round things?

Are they nuts? Are they balls? No. They are armadillos! The three-banded armadillo (ar muh DIH loh) can roll into a ball. It is safe inside its shell.

Can all armadillos roll up into balls?
How can they do it?

All armadillos curl up when danger nears. But the three-banded armadillo is the only kind that can make a tight ball.

When the armadillo is poked, its shell snaps shut like a trap. The armadillo can do this because the front and back of its shell are not attached to its skin on the sides. There is plenty of space inside the shell for the animal's head, legs, and tail.

Can an animal borrow a shell?

A hermit crab does not have its own shell. It finds one left by another animal. It moves in. The crab is safe inside its new shell.

▶

How do hermit crabs stay safe?

Sharks, rays, and large fish will eat a hermit crab if they get the chance. To stay safe from those predators, the hermit crab finds another animal's shell and crawls into it. But one shell will not last a lifetime. As the hermit crab grows, it gets too big for its old shell. It must find a new, larger shell to call home.

How do herds keep animals safe?

These animals are called blackbucks. Many blackbucks live together in a **herd**. Living in a group helps them stay safe.

Why is there safety in numbers?

This blackbuck mother and her calf are alone at the water hole. They are in danger because they are by themselves. A wolf could attack them.

Soon, they will go back to join their herd. In a big group, they will be safer. Many pairs of eyes and ears will be alert to danger. The herd will run away together if a wolf comes close.

Will a fish eat this sea slug?

Sea slugs live in the ocean. There is **poison** in its body. Its bright colors warn fish to stay away. The colors say, "Do not eat me! I will make you sick."

▶

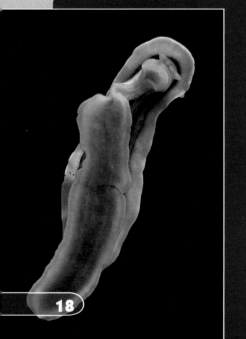

What is warning coloration?

Some animals have bright colors or patterns. They do not blend with their background. They are very easy for predators to see. So what keeps them safe?

These bright animals contain poisons that taste bad. For example, a fish that might eat a sea slug will try only once. It will spit the slug out. It learns to stay away from the slug's bright colors.

18

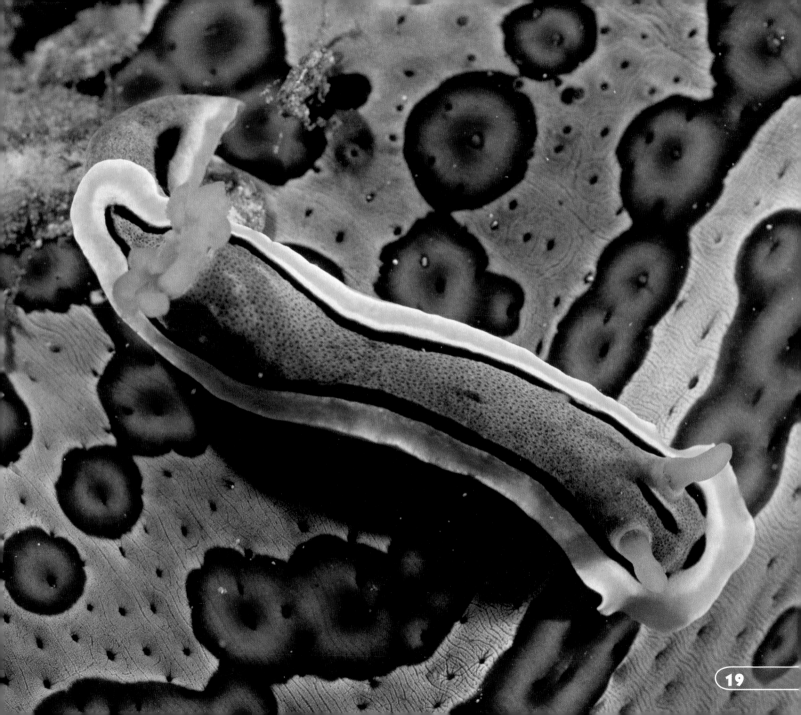

What are these doves doing?

These doves look dead. They are not. The birds are "playing dead" to fool their enemies. When danger passes, they will move again.

What good is pretending?

Doves are not the only animals that "play dead" to fool predators. Rabbits do it. Many insects do it, too.

"Playing dead" works because many predators only go after prey that moves. They pass by an animal that stays still. It is a puzzle why predators lose interest in an "easy meal."

How can a butterfly look scary?

Watch out! This big, scary eye is watching you! Were you fooled? This is not an eye. It is a spot on a butterfly's wing. The eyespots scare away birds that might eat the butterfly. ▶

How do eyespots keep butterflies safe?

Many butterflies have big eyespots on their back wings. When the butterfly sits still, its front wings cover the spots. When a predator approaches, the butterfly suddenly shows the spots. The scared predator goes away.

Some butterflies have little eyespots on the edges of their wings. A predator mistakes an eyespot for an insect. It attacks, but it gets only a small bite of the wing. The butterfly stays safe.

What is hiding in this picture?

◀ This leaf insect looks like the leaves it sits on. Other animals do not see it. They do not eat it.

How does disguise help animals stay safe?

One way to escape predators is to look like something else. This leaf insect lives on guava (GWAH vuh) trees. It looks like a guava leaf. When it is still, it is almost impossible to see.

When it walks, it moves its body gently back and forth. It looks like a leaf swaying in the breeze. Its disguise is so good, it can move around in daylight and not be eaten by birds.

What is this fish doing?

Danger is near! The pufferfish blows up like a balloon. Its spines stick out. It looks big and mean. No other fish eats it. ▶

How do pufferfish puff up?

Most of the time, a pufferfish is small. But when a predator is near, the pufferfish can swell to three times its normal size. It fills its stomach with water. Its skin and spines push out as water enters.

How does puffing keep the fish safe? Maybe the blown-up pufferfish looks too scary for predators to attack. Or maybe it is too hard to bite or swallow! No one knows for sure.

What good are a porcupine's quills?

Porcupines are covered in **quills**. The quills are long and pointy. An enemy comes near. The porcupine stands still. It raises its quills. It shakes its quills. The enemy runs away.

How does a porcupine use its quills to stay safe?

Some people think porcupines can shoot their quills like darts. That is not true. When the porcupine is threatened, it rattles its quills and shows them to its attacker.

Porcupines can back into a predator. The sharp quills are loose in the porcupine's skin. The quills may stick into an enemy and fall off the porcupine.

29

Learn More

Books

Clarke, Ginjer L. *Fake Out!: Animals That Play Tricks*. New York: Grosset and Dunlap, 2007.

Guidoux, Valérie. *Hidden Animals*. Ontario, Canada: Firefly, 2006.

Weber, Belinda. *Animal Disguises*. Boston: Kingfisher, 2004.

Whitehouse, Patricia. *Hiding in a Desert*. Chicago: Heinemann, 2003.

Web Sites

Enchanted Learning. "Camouflaged Animals."
http://www.zoomschool.com/coloring/camouflage.shtml

National Geographic Kids.
http://kids.nationalgeographic.com/animals/

Index

Special thanks to Dr. Martin Stevens, Department of Zoology, Cambridge University, England, for his expert assistance.

Enslow Elementary, an imprint of Enslow Publishers, Inc.

Enslow Elementary® is a registered trademark of Enslow Publishers, Inc.

Copyright © 2010 by Enslow Publishers, Inc.

Library of Congress Cataloging-in-Publication Data

Brynie, Faith Hickman, 1946–

 How do animals stay safe? / Faith Hickman Brynie.

    p. cm. — (I like reading about animals!)

 Includes bibliographical references and index.

 Summary: "Leveled reader that explains how different animals defend themselves and stay safe in both first grade text and third grade text"—Provided by publisher.

 ISBN 978-0-7660-3326-9

 1. Animal defenses—Juvenile literature. I. Title.

 QL759.B79 2010

 591.47—dc22

                          2008050058

 ISBN-13: 978-0-7660-3747-2 (paperback ed.)

Printed in the United States of America

112009 Lake Book Manufacturing, Inc., Melrose Park, IL

10 9 8 7 6 5 4 3 2 1

Photo Credits: Photos by naturepl.com: © Bernard Castelein, p. 17; © Constantinos Petrinos, pp. 26, 32; © Doug Perrine, pp. 9, 15; © Elio Della Ferrera, p. 16; © George McCarthy, p. 5; © Ingo Arndt, p. 1; © Georgette Douwma, pp. 8, 14; © Jeff Rotman, pp. 1, 27; © John Downer Productions, p. 20; © Mark Payne-Gill, pp. 12, 13; © Michael D. Kern, p. 22; © Phil Savoie, pp. 4, 23; © Rod Williams, pp. 28, 30–31; © Solvin Zankl, pp. 18, 19; © Staffan Widstrand, p. 7; © Studio Times Ltd, pp. 24, 25; © Tom Vezo, p. 11; © Tony Heald, pp. 21, 29. **Photo by Shutterstock,** pp. 2–3.

Cover Photo: © Ingo Arndt/naturepl.com

Series Science Consultant:
Helen Hess, PhD
Professor of Biology
College of the Atlantic
Bar Harbor, ME

Series Literacy Consultant:
Allan A. De Fina, PhD
Dean, College of Education/Professor of Literacy Education
New Jersey City University
Past President of the New Jersey Reading Association

Enslow Elementary
an imprint of
 Enslow Publishers, Inc.
40 Industrial Road
Box 398
Berkeley Heights, NJ 07922
USA
http://www.enslow.com